D1402995

It's Challah Time!

Latifa Berry Kropf

photographs by Tod Cohen

Kar-Ben Publishing

Thank you. . .

Children of Beth Israel Congregation Preschool for your cooperation, enthusiasm and delightfulness. We couldn't have done this without you. Thanks also to your parents for their support in this project.

Alice, for sharing yourself with us every Friday. We believe you are one of the *Lamed Vovniks* who keep the world going.

Cantor Allen, for the *ruach* you bring to our Friday mornings and the way you help us "bring in the Shabbat."

Sharia, for the loving presence you have been in our classroom.

Peter, for all the technical assistance and for easing our way through cyberspace.

Ellen, for your enthusiasm and eager support in the making of this book.

John, for your wisdom, guidance, and hand-holding.

L.B.K.

Text copyright © 2002 by Latifa Berry Kropf
Photos copyright © 2002 by Tod Cohen

Kar-Ben Publishing, Inc.
A division of Lerner Publishing Group
241 First Avenue North
Minneapolis, MN 55401 U.S.A.
1-800-4-KARBEN

Website address: www.karben.com

Library of Congress Cataloging-in-Publication Data

Kropf, Latifa Berry.
     It's challah time! / by Latifa Berry Kropf ; photos by Tod Cohen.
        p.   cm.
     Summary: A photo essay which follows preschoolers in a
Jewish nursery school as they make challah, the braided
bread eaten on Shabbat, the Jewish Sabbath.
     ISBN: 1–58013–036–4 (lib. bdg. : alk. paper)
     1. Cookery, Jewish—Juvenile literature. [1. Cookery, Jewish.
2. Sabbath.] I. Cohen, Tod, ill. II. Title.
TX724 .K77 2002
641.5'676—dc21   2002000443

Manufactured in the United States of America
1 2 3 4 5 6 – JR – 08 07 06 05 04 03

Today is Friday.
Time to make challah for Shabbat.

First we need lots of flour.

Then we add yeast to make it rise . . .
and cinnamon and honey to make it sweet.

Crack! In go the eggs.

Then we mix, mix, mix.

And knead to make it smooth.

The dough has been resting and growing.
Soon it will be ready to be made into loaves.

Rebecca is rolling the dough into three snakes.

And Josh is braiding them together.

The loaves are ready to bake.
Sprinkle, sprinkle, sprinkle.
Josh likes cinnamon and sugar on his challah.

Goodbye, challah. Time to go to the oven.

While the challah is baking
Rebecca and her friends are sharing a book . . .

and Cantor Allen is teaching us Shabbat songs.

Todah rabah*, Dena, for setting the table
for our Shabbat party.

*Thank you

The challah is finished baking.
It's warm and brown and ready to eat.

Let's cover it and place it on the table
with the candles and grape juice.

We sing the blessing and light the candles,
bringing the light into ourselves.

Then we sing a blessing and sip some juice.
Shabbat tastes sweet.

Uncover the challah. It feels so warm.
Let's sing the blessing and taste our bread.

Yum!

Whole Wheat Honey Challah

2 Tbsp. yeast
$\frac{1}{2}$ cup warm water
1 tsp. honey

4 cups whole wheat flour
$\frac{1}{2}$ cup oil
$\frac{1}{2}$ cup honey (less the teaspoon mixed with the yeast)

2 eggs
2 tsp. salt
1 Tbsp. cinnamon
1 Tbsp. vanilla
$1\frac{1}{2}$ cups warm water

Up to 3 cups white flour
Poppy seeds, sesame seeds, or cinnamon/sugar mixture for top

In a small bowl, mix yeast with $\frac{1}{2}$ cup warm water, and a bit of the honey. Let it bubble.

In a large bowl, mix the wheat flour, oil, eggs, salt, cinnamon, vanilla, and the rest of the honey. Add the yeast mixture and $1\frac{1}{2}$ cups warm water. Add the white flour one cup at a time and when the dough is firm, begin kneading it. Add more white flour as needed. The dough should not be sticky.

Put the dough in an oiled bowl and cover it with a damp cloth. Let it rise for one hour.

Punch down the dough to remove the air bubbles. Form loaves. This recipe makes four large loaves or two large loaves to eat in school and a dozen small loaves for children to take home.

Place the loaves on cookie sheets that have been oiled or covered with parchment. Sprinkle with a topping of your choice.

Bake in a preheated oven at 325 degrees for 20 minutes. (Little loaves need only about 12 minutes.) Place on a rack to cool . . . and enjoy!

This recipe can be cut in half and can also be made in a bread machine.

BLESSINGS

Over the candles

בָּרוּךְ אַתָּה יְיָ אֱלֹהֵינוּ מֶלֶךְ הָעוֹלָם,
אֲשֶׁר קִדְּשָׁנוּ בְּמִצְוֹתָיו וְצִוָּנוּ לְהַדְלִיק נֵר שֶׁל שַׁבָּת.

Baruch Atah Adonai Eloheinu Melech ha'olam,
asher kid'shanu b'mitzvotav v'tzivanu l'hadlik ner shel Shabbat.

Blessed are You, our God, Ruler of the world, who has made us holy,
and has given us the mitzvah of lighting the Shabbat candles.

Over the wine

בָּרוּךְ אַתָּה יְיָ אֱלֹהֵינוּ מֶלֶךְ הָעוֹלָם, בּוֹרֵא פְּרִי הַגָּפֶן.

Baruch Atah Adonai Eloheinu Melech ha'olam, borei p'ri hagafen.

Blessed are You, our God, Ruler of the world,
who has created the fruit of the vine.

Over the bread

בָּרוּךְ אַתָּה יְיָ אֱלֹהֵינוּ מֶלֶךְ הָעוֹלָם, הַמּוֹצִיא לֶחֶם מִן הָאָרֶץ.

Baruch Atah Adonai Eloheinu Melech ha'olam, hamotzi lechem min ha'aretz.

Blessed are You, our God, Ruler of the world,
who gives us bread from the earth.